KW-221-600

CONTENTS

4

THE SHOW MUST GO ON

By Richard O'Neill and Michelle Russell

Illustrated by Mitch Miller

Published by Pearson Education Limited, 80 Strand, London, WC2R 0RL.

www.pearsonschools.co.uk

Text © Pearson Education Limited 2021
Designed and typeset by Collaborate Agency
Edited by Hannah Hirst-Dunton
Produced by Oriel Square
Original illustrations © Pearson Education Limited 2021
Illustrated by Mitch Miller
Cover design by Collaborate Agency
Cover illustration © Pearson Education Limited 2021

First published 2021

24 23 22 21
10 9 8 7 6 5 4 3 2 1

British Library Cataloguing in Publication Data
A catalogue record for this book is available from the British Library

ISBN 978 1 292 37241 9

Printed in the UK by Ashford Press Ltd.

Acknowledgements
We would like to thank the children and teachers of Thorntree Primary School, Glasgow, as well as Christine Stirling from The Showmen's Guild for their invaluable help in the development of this title.

The author and publisher would like to thank the following individuals for permission to reproduce photographs: Photographer - Adam Russell; Model - Robert Miller.

Note from the publisher
Pearson has robust editorial processes, including answer and fact checks, to ensure the accuracy of the content in this publication, and every effort is made to ensure this publication is free of errors. We are, however, only human, and occasionally errors do occur. Pearson is not liable for any misunderstandings that arise as a result of errors in this publication, but it is our priority to ensure that the content is accurate. If you spot an error, please do contact us at resourcescorrections@ pearson.com so we can make sure it is corrected.

Chapter One

GRANDAD'S TREASURE

Nestled quietly by the railway and the river, in the Showman's Yard, a treasure trove can be found … but only by those who really look, and really listen.

"Not all treasure glistens," said Grandad, with a twinkle in his eye.

I smiled back at Grandad and watched him hang an old chairoplane swing on the hook beside the door of his shed, just under a big blue 'Hook-A-Duck' sign that was missing a few letters. Every space was filled with something that could be useful, and Grandad always knew exactly where to find what he needed.

From the outside of the shed, you'd never guess what treasures lay within. It had once been a box truck – like a big trailer that was waiting to be hitched to a cab and ready to travel. It hadn't moved for a long time, though.

Its side could be lifted all the way up to make a roof, and the floor folded out to make a big workspace. Grandad used the extra space to fix rides and stalls during the winter. During the summer, Nana liked using it as a shady place to read a good book.

6

I loved listening to Grandad tell
stories about the treasures he had
in his big shed. There, he was like a
magician, able to fix almost anything.
Now he was
showing me what
his new project
would be.

GRANDAD

NANA

With a loud 'THWUMP', Grandad pulled down a heavy canvas cover to reveal what we'd been looking for: a dusty old wooden galloper horse that had once been part of the carousel. It wobbled and toppled towards us – and we caught it just before it hit the floor.

SASH TO PAINT
SOMEONE'S NAME ON

CANVAS
TILT
TO
PROTECT
IT

Giving a cheeky wink, Grandad chuckled, "This might look like an ordinary horse – but it's going to have an extraordinary job!"

Chapter Two

MY FAMILY

Grandad is a Showman. He has lots of treasure hidden away in his shed, but he says his most precious treasure is our family.

My name is Mary Ann. During the colder months, I live in our family's home yard on Jane Street, right next to the allotments, with Grandad Henry and Nana Sylvia. In the summer, the yard is mostly a wide-open space – but in the winter, it's filled with aunties, uncles, lots of cousins and me, Mam, Dad, my big brother Ross and our big sister Hannah.

ME!

MAM

DAD

↑ ROSS

HANNAH

OUR YARD

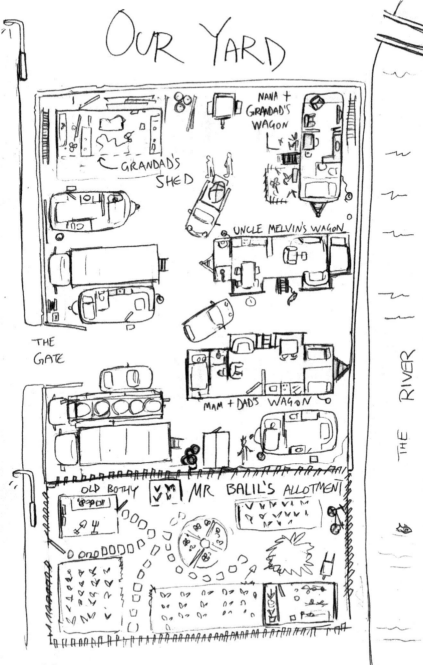

Like us, Nana and Grandad used to travel to towns and cities, building up the big rides and side stalls ready for the excited children to spend their pocket money. Now they stay in our yard all year 'round because of Nana's health. When we're home, we help Nana and Grandad to keep our yard tidy, put the big bins by the gate every Thursday and sort the letters that appear in our big metal post-box.

Grandad is still a member of the Showmen's Guild, which helps to organise the fairs that my family and my cousins visit all over the country. He's also busy making a new ride – I can't wait to see it!

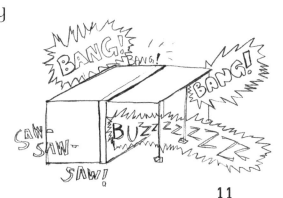

11

My cousin Tia is two days older than me.

She lives with the twins, Macy and Maxwell, in a house near the yard. She doesn't travel like me, as her mam (my Auntie Mary) chose to settle and works in the local hospital. They get to see Nana and Grandad every day.

Nana keeps Macy and Maxwell entertained with one of her treasure boxes – an old biscuit tin filled with buttons, old pennies and other bits and bobs. Each trinket in the treasure tin has a story and Nana is always ready to tell us these stories while sipping a nice cup of tea.

Nana let me have some of the old photos and stamps out of another treasure tin for my scrapbook.

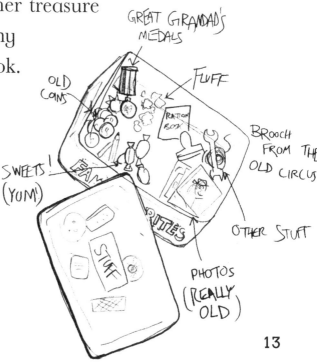

GREAT GRANDAD'S MEDALS

OLD COINS

FLUFF

RATION BOOK

BROOCH FROM THE OLD CIRCUS

SWEETS! (YUM!)

OTHER STUFF

PHOTOS (REALLY OLD)

STUFF

13

Chapter Three

SUMMER SEASON

During the summer, while the fairs are out travelling, I sometimes don't see my cousins for months – not until we come back to Jane Street.

My older cousins, Felix and Big Jimmy, help my Uncle Melvin with the big wheel and the dodgems. They're always busy when building up the rides and stalls, making sure the people who visit have fun and stay safe.

UNCLE MELVIN

BIG JIMMY

FELIX

Their mam, Auntie May, manages the paybox. If we're at the same fair, I'm allowed to sit with her and watch her count the money.

Knowing how to sort the coins will be really useful when our class gets to run the school tuck shop next year!

NOTES STACKED IN 100s

COUNTED CHANGE GOES IN MONEYBAGS

MONEY POCKETS

Throughout the season, Hannah, Ross and I get to see all kinds of other things, too. We learn all about how our family sets up the prizes, minds the stalls and tests the rides. Hannah already knows how to fix the lightbulbs on the arcades.

I especially love watching Mam make the sweet treats, making sure that we have everything we need for the candyfloss, which lots of children like. They can buy it on a stick or in a bag. My mam makes the best toffee apples, too: shiny, bright red and sticky. They look like giant lollipops standing in a row.

Once everything's set up, just like the children from the village or town, we have lots of fun playing on all the different stalls and rides – but we don't have to pay!

We have to remember to do our school work when we're away, too, so Mam sets up a little table in our living wagon.

MISS PHAM MY TEACHER

I keep this scrapbook as a diary as well. My teacher likes looking at it and learning about all the shows we put on. She says I have the know-how to help her plan the school Winter Fair! Grandad said we can borrow some of our old side-stall games, like the ring toss and coconut shy, too.

My cousin Tia is in the same class as me, and we always sit together. Hannah and Ross send their schoolwork through the internet, though, so I have to be careful not to delete anything off the laptop.

That's why I like doing my writing in my scrapbook – nothing ever gets deleted and I can still work on it when there's no internet connection.

When it's time for the fair to move on, all the grown-ups pull it down again and pack it up, so it's ready for the next place that's waiting for its thrills and excitement. Then, once the season is over, we travel back to our yard. Nana and Grandad always welcome us back with a great big hug and tasty roast dinner. They always look forward to the stories that I've got to tell about my travels.

Chapter Four

TROUBLE OVER THE WATER

Opposite Jane Street, beyond the railway track, on the other side of the river, the windows of tall apartment blocks shine. That's where my friend Millie lives. Her bedroom window has blue blinds and is right above the lamp post.

I think the apartment buildings are quite pretty. If you squint your eyes just a little, they look like they're covered in lots of televisions – a hundred movies playing at once.

MY FRIEND MILLIE

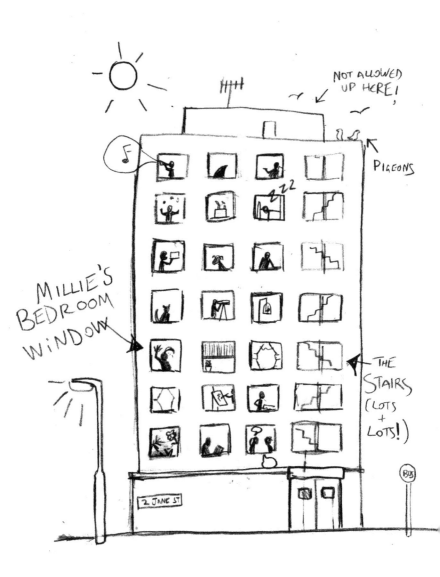

Unlike us on our street, Millie doesn't know everyone who lives in her apartment block. She only really knows her next-door neighbour, Miss Andrews, who owns three pocket-sized dogs. I sometimes see them when they go for a walk along the river.

POCKET-SIZED DOGS

When I visited Millie and looked out of her window, I could see the river and most of our street, including a bit of our yard and our neighbour Mr Balil's allotment next door. Millie says she likes the view, but last week we learned that not everyone agrees with her.

The news was on the telly in Nana's wagon when she suddenly turned up the sound. We watched closely as the report showed a video of our yard and Mr Balil's allotment – just like what I could see from Millie's side of the river! I thought it was exciting, but then the presenter

announced "plans to build on the site over the water, which the developers have described as a 'junkyard' and an 'eyesore'".

That was our street she was talking about! What a cheek: we don't live in a junkyard!

I stomped down the steps of the wagon and kicked the stones as I walked along the path. I looked around Grandad's shed and I accidently kicked the old galloper. A fragment of paint fell onto my shoe. I looked into the horse's chipped face and it somehow seemed to be laughing at me. Maybe it was junk after all.

When I headed back out into the yard, all the grown-ups were asking lots of questions.

"Where would we go?"

"What could we do?"

Chapter Five

THE IMPORTANT CLIPBOARD

Yesterday, a man with an important clipboard came to visit. He listened to the adults and he wrote things down. He told the grown-ups that the apartment-building company might be able to persuade the council to carry out something called a 'compulsory purchase order'. He said it would let them buy the land that our yard and Mr Balil's allotment was on – even if we didn't want them to! That would mean we couldn't live here any more.

IMPORTANT CLIPBOARD)

"Where would we go?"

"What could we do?"

The grown-ups asked more questions. Ross and I gave the man our best hard stares, but he didn't seem to notice.

Then my eyes started to blink quickly and I could see lots of little stars. I uncrossed my arms and gave Grandad a big hug.

As the man with the important clipboard went away, Grandad ruffled my brother's hair and gave me a wink that meant 'Don't worry, I'm sure we can fix this.' That made me feel a whole lot better.

Chapter Six

SOS!

The next day, we painted some big signs to tell other people about the terrible threat to Jane Street. Uncle Melvin insisted that we all paint **'SOS'** signs. My cousin was confused at first, but I remembered doing a project on Morse code. I knew that 'SOS' meant someone needed help. Our SOS had an extra special meaning:

Save Our Street!

"It's a great idea, Uncle Melvin," I grinned.

Meanwhile, Nana hunted out some old papers and photographs. They were of the land before the yard was built. She carefully unfolded a newspaper clipping of three men holding shovels. The headline said **'NEW FAMILY ARRIVES WITH A BANG!'**

Nana told us that no-one else wanted this land all those years ago and that, after the war, her great-grandfather Ray and his brothers had to get their army friends from the bomb disposal unit to detonate the unexploded bombs to make the land safe. It was a good place to spend the winter, near enough to the roads that led to the places we still visit with our shows.

"Maybe we could try to show people our history here," she suggested.

As we looked at more photographs, we could see the old rides. The galloper, sitting in the shed with its peeling paint, was shown in its former glory. It looked beautiful.

Grandad was right: the bits and bobs he'd saved in his shed weren't pieces of junk. They were ready to perform – ready to make the show go on! They were ready to show the world that, like us, they were extraordinary – that they could bring smiles and fun wherever they might travel.

That night, I tossed and turned in bed. My mind was full of gallopers and dodgems, candyfloss and bright lights.

When I woke up, I had a plan.

Chapter Seven

PLAN OF ACTION

We picked up the paintbrushes, which Uncle Melvin had cleaned the night before. The brushes did a fabulous job: each stroke was vibrant, waking up the galloper – bringing him back to life.

That was my plan: to bring everything in the yard back to life and put on a show right there, rather than taking it on the road. We were going to remind people about the excitement and importance of fairgrounds, and the people who create them.

Uncle Melvin smiled and we watched him carefully paint 'Reminiscence' on the wooden sash that swished below the horse's mane.

"That means 'remembering'," he said with a grin.

"A fitting name for a fine animal," laughed Nana. I agreed – Reminiscence was soon going to help us share our memories and stories with everyone!

Nana set up some tables under the side roof of Grandad's shed, covering them with some big pieces of brightly coloured material. It was the perfect setting for her scrapbooks and trinkets. She pegged some photographs on the string she had tied up.

Grandad and Uncle Melvin hunted out the old game boards, and Dad helped to set up some little tables for them. They were making a row of stalls leading up to Nana's display, just like the ones we used to lead fair-goers to the big, adventurous rides.

Mam and Felix made some beanbags out of old clothes, and Auntie Mary came to the yard with coconuts, hoops and other things she thought we might need. Mr Balil from the allotment next door brought some plants for Nana to display. Then Mam organised for Grandad's new ride – the Starflyer – to be built between our Showman's yard and Mr Balil's allotment. It looked magnificent.

It was just like building up a show, but this time we were setting it up at home, all together.

Chapter Eight

ROLL UP! ROLL UP!

Everything was ready. Lots of people had seen our posters and signs. A journalist from the local newspaper had also interviewed Nana and Grandad.

We were headline news!

Although we don't really say 'roll up, roll up', that was the headline the newspaper chose to use. Nana said that a lot of movies and stories include Showmen shouting this out to attract crowds of people, so it'd be familiar – and we wanted lots of people to visit our yard.

ROLL UP! ROLL UP!

Interview with local Showmen and Activists

We made sure everything was safe. Each adult had their own job helping the visitors to have fun.

Dad had found some new plastic letters for the big blue 'Hook-A-Duck' sign and Uncle Melvin had fixed it to a board.

Beside the fence, all the old Noah's Ark animals had been gathered like a little wooden zoo – Big Jimmy had spent hours making a little platform for each animal, so they stood upright.

Hannah made sure that the tin cans were steady, with the newly made beanbags waiting for someone to throw.

The water in the middle of the 'Hook-A-Duck' stall started to settle, and the ducks became as still as the hook poles, which were standing to attention and ready for action.

The candyfloss machine was heating up, ready for the swirls of candyfloss to be twirled around wooden sticks by Mam.

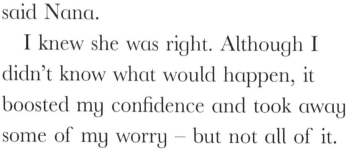

"Whatever happens, every one of us has done our best," said Nana.

I knew she was right. Although I didn't know what would happen, it boosted my confidence and took away some of my worry – but not all of it.

Chapter Nine

THE FUN OF THE FAIR

Reminiscence the galloping horse stood proud as he waited to greet the curious visitors through our gate into the yard – our home. His bright colours shone like a rainbow, bringing instant smiles to faces of children as they excitedly led their grown-ups into the yard.

Millie and Miss Andrews waved to other people who lived in their apartments as they watched the old pennies roll down the chute.

Millie chose the shiniest coin and placed it in the groove at the top. As it rolled towards the numbers, she held her breath as she waited to see where it would land.

A chorus of laughter and cheers could be heard as a coconut was knocked off its shy.

The tin cans rattled and rolled as a beanbag hit its target, while the ducks bobbed up and down, teasing the hooks that hovered above them.

It was like a big party where everyone wanted to be. All of the grown-up visitors chatted and laughed as they shared stories of when they were little and of their favourite fairground games. Hidden treasure and childhood memories were being rediscovered.

Even the news reporter and her camera crew came. They said the views from the top of the Starflyer were amazing. I knew they'd never think of our home as a junkyard again!

My idea for Saving Our Street was really working!

NEWS
REPORTER

Chapter Ten

TIME TO REST

Nestled quietly by the railway and the river, in the Showman's Yard, a treasure trove has been found … because the people who had visited it had really looked and had really listened!

I smile as I cut out the newspaper article that celebrates our achievement, with the proud headline 'JANE STREET SAVED!'

JANE STREET SAVED!

Looking at the photograph reminds me of looking into one of Nana's treasure tins.

I grin at all the people, with their smiles shining brightly from the black-and-white picture. So many people had visited and helped with our SOS that the council had seen how important it was for us to stay! Not everyone can be seen in the photograph, but I can remember all the laughter and chatter that filled our yard.

Most of our treasures are now back in storage, having fulfilled their mission to Save Our Street. The little trinket box with its bright pennies, the black-and-white photographs of days gone by and the galloper with colours so bright are hiding out of sight again – in just the right places, where Grandad can find them next time.

Some of the treasures get to travel with Nana, though. She visits the local schools and library to talk about the travelling Showmen and their adventures around the country.

Now she has a new story to tell, too, about how our yard brought people together. Millie's made lots of new friends in her building, and Mr Balil's shared the vegetables from his allotment: he's given our Hannah a box of parsnips, and parcelled up the rest for Miss Andrews to cook in her apartment.

I stick the newspaper cutting into my scrapbook, close my eyes and listen to the peace and quiet that surround Jane Street Yard and Allotments once more. Well, it's almost quiet – Grandad is still busy in his shed.

Then, from the path by the gate, I hear a little cry. Little Jimmy, another of Millie's neighbours, has dropped his toy truck and broken off the wheel.

Kneeling on the ground beside Jimmy and his toy, I give a little wink and say, "Don't worry – Grandad will fix it. It may seem like an ordinary truck now, but it can still do an extraordinary job!"

And, taking my hand, Jimmy carries the little toy truck over towards Grandad's shed.

MEET SHOWMAN ROBERT MILLER

How long have you lived on your yard?

I've been here for about 54 years, since I was little. My parents leased the land from the council when we could no longer stay on our old yard because of road developments. Years later, my wife and I bought the land and now we live here all year. My family lives in the yard too!

Where is your favourite place in your yard?

I like spending time in my truck, which is like a big storeroom. It's where I do lots of repairing and painting. I started to learn how to paint and sign-write as a boy, by watching my family use different brushes. Some of the brushes I use now are very old and were passed down to me through my family.